FELLOWSHIP *of* PRAYER

LENTEN DEVOTIONAL 2016

The Way of Dreams and Visions

by Sarah Griffith Lund

CHALICE PRESS

ST. LOUIS, MISSOURI

An imprint of Christian Board of Publication

Print: 9780827211100 • EPUB: 9780827211117
EPDF Read Only: 9780827211124 • EPDF Printable: 9780827211131

www.chalicepress.com

About the Author

Sarah Griffith Lund is passionate about loving her family and God, and being part of faith communities. She is a Vice President for Seminary Advancement for Christian Theological Seminary in Indianapolis, and has served as pastor to churches in Brooklyn, N.Y., Minneapolis, and New Smyrna Beach, Fla. The author of *Blessed Are the Crazy:Breaking the Silence about Mental Illness, Family, and Church,* she blogs at sarahgriffithlund.com and at huffingtonpost.com.

Dear Readers,

The world spins in time and space, moving through the universe God created in the very beginning. Genesis tells us that on the first day, God dreamed Creation into being and God's vision of a new heaven and new earth was born. Dreams and visions have inspired both divine and human activity since the beginning of time. The Bible reflects the dreams and visions of the ancient prophets, kings and queens, and inspired contemporary prophets such as the Rev. Dr. Martin Luther King Jr. to proclaim to a racially and economically divided nation: "I have a dream."

In the seasonal cycles of winter, spring, summer, and fall, we experience the birth and death and rebirth of creation all around us. The life of Christian faith echoes these seasons in the birth, life, death, and resurrection of Jesus. These seasons of the natural world and the spiritual world converge in the spring, inviting those seeking to follow Jesus into a time for deeper reflection on the magnitude of how dreams and visions shape our seasons of life: birth, life, death, and rebirth. The season of Lent, culminating in Holy Week, is a special time set apart for disciples today to engage in deep theological reflection. In an age of climate crisis, we can observe a parallel crisis of faith. Where is God to be known, encountered, and embodied in these turbulent times? How is God revealed in our dreams and visions, becoming known to us in the night?

Now is the time for Christian communities to boldly reclaim the radical message of our faith: God's original dream where all of Creation is good and Jesus' vision of a world where love, justice, and mercy rule the day. We are promised the gift of the Holy Spirit to empower our boldness. If we are to succeed in revitalizing our faith and giving emerging generations faithful ways of being in the world, we must first be rooted in the Spirit, connected daily to the living Christ and firmly planted in God, the ground of our being.

First proclaimed by the Hebrew Prophet Joel (Joel 2:28) and echoed in the New Testament letter by the Apostle Paul are these words:

'In the last days it will be, God declares,
that I will pour out my Spirit upon all flesh,
and your sons and your daughters shall prophesy,
and your young men shall see visions." (Acts 2:17)

In this *Fellowship of Prayer,* we journey together through the season of Lent, opening ourselves up to be inspired by the dreams and visions in scripture. This Lenten season, we ask the question and discern together: How can our lives reflect the audacious dreams and transformational visions that God has for each one of us, for our communities of faith, and for all of Creation?

Sarah Griffith Lund

Seeing Visions of God

Read Ezekiel 1:1–14.

In my thirtieth year, in the fourth month on the fifth day, while I was among the exiles by the Kebar River, the heavens were opened and I saw visions of God. (Ezekiel 1:1, NIV)

One of the threads that ties together the entire biblical narrative from Genesis to Revelation is the ongoing encounter between God and humankind. God chooses to be revealed to us through dreams and visions, and the Hebrew prophetic priest Ezekiel is no exception. The profound vision carried throughout the book of Ezekiel occurs during a time of political unrest, exile, and uncertainty for the people of Israel. Into this great time of despair, God speaks a word of challenge and hope through the visionary leader. This experience is known as a "theophany," when God shows up.

Leaders who are led by God will be risk takers, led by God's vision. As we begin the season of Lent, we are mindful of the many dreams and visions that we have wasted, that have burned like coals, and faded away because of our lack of attention and care. We mourn the death of our dreams. Like Ezekiel, wherever we are positioned—as a priest, a homemaker, a teacher, or a leader—on Ash Wednesday we see ourselves through the lens of exile. We have left the homeland of the vision of God's realm; we have abandoned God's dream. Through our own inaction, we have failed to faithfully tend one another's dreams, we have failed to protect the earth. The dream of Eden escapes us. Today we confess the ways, big and small, that we have turned away from God. We confess that we are exiled from God's dreams and visions for the church and the world.

Prayer: God, forgive us for failing to catch, hold onto, and nurture the dreams and visions you give us. Give our leaders hearts and minds receptive to the vision from heaven so that through the church the world may be renewed. Help us to make time to dream. Amen.

God's Promise: Rainbows on a Rainy Day

Read Ezekiel 1:15–28.

Like the appearance of a rainbow in the clouds on a rainy day, so was the radiance around him. This was the appearance of the likeness of the glory of the LORD. When I saw it, I fell facedown, and I heard the voice of one speaking. (Ezekiel 1:28, NIV)

Ezekiel's vivid descriptions of his vision of wheeled and winged creatures surrounded by fire invite us to wonder what this is all about. Is Ezekiel crazy? Did he have an undiagnosed psychiatric disorder that caused him to hallucinate? We read that Ezekiel's response to this vision was to fall "facedown" (1:28). A few verses later we learn that it was through this vision of the glory of the Lord that God called Ezekiel into ministry.

It's not by accident that Ezekiel saw "a rainbow in the clouds on a rainy day" (1:28). Before God calls Ezekiel to ministry, God reminds him of the promise represented in the rainbow: "I have set my rainbow in the clouds, and it will be the sign of the covenant between me and the earth" (Genesis 9:13, NIV). Even while the last raindrops fall from the great flood, God sends a sign of God's commitment to be in relationship with the earth.

Like seeing a rainbow on a rainy day, we can catch glimpses of God's promise to us. The rainbow comes to us only after the sun's view is hidden from our sight, its light clouded and distant. Yet if we look with the spiritual eyes of our heart, we can see that visions of God are all around us, even on cloudy days. Sometimes it is on the dreariest of days that God breaks through to us.

Prayer: God of the rainbow, thank you for your promise to be in relationship with us. As you did for Ezekiel, show us a visible sign of your divine presence, appear to us in your radiance, and let us hear your voice. Amen.

Lifted by the Spirit, Led by the Lord

Read Ezekiel 11:16–25.

The spirit lifted me up and brought me in a vision by the spirit of God into Chaldea, to the exiles. Then the vision that I had seen left me. And I told the exiles all the things that the LORD had shown me. (Ezekiel 11:24–25)

Dreams and visions lift us from what is now to what is possible in the future. To lead transformative change, we need dreamers and visionaries to imagine different realities. This is the role of the prophet, the person who sees with God's eyes a new heaven and a new earth.

What was it like for the exiles who listened to Ezekiel as he told them of "all the things that the LORD had shown me" (11:25)? Did they question his authority or wonder if they could trust his intentions? Or were his words like sweet honey for a people in exile, a time of bitterness and loss? The prophet recalls for them God's promise: "They shall be my people, and I will be their God" (11:20).

Dreamers and visionaries are people lifted by the Spirit and led by the Lord. Ezekiel's role in the faith community is to be a conduit for divine intervention; God's will is made known through him. The dreams and visions are intended to be shared for the benefit and uplifting of the community—not for personal gain or profit. We are wise to discern whether our religious leaders are promoting themselves, advocating for their own ego-driven success, or if they are really about the work of advancing God's new heaven and new earth. We want to see the prophetic leaders of our day lifted by the Spirit and led by the Lord.

Prayer: God of the dreamers and visionaries, lift us up by your Spirit and lead us by your divine grace. Show us all that you would have us dream into being so that the world may be made new and whole in love. Whatever new thing you are calling us to see, open our eyes. Amen.

Visions from the Valley

Read Ezekiel 37:1–6.

The hand of the Lord came upon me, and he brought me out by the spirit of the Lord and set me down in the middle of a valley; it was full of bones. He led me all around them; there were very many lying in the valley, and they were very dry. He said to me, "Mortal, can these bones live?" I answered, "O Lord God, you know." (Ezekiel 37:1–3)

One afternoon walking in our neighborhood, my preschooler and I made a discovery: a small animal skull. After a good rinsing and bleaching, it became a conversation piece for our family. What kind of animal was it? How old was it? How did it die? Bones have a way of eliciting searching questions. What if the bones could talk?

Ezekiel's vision of the valley of dry bones haunts us because of both the context and the content of the passage. Brittle human bones and this question confront him: "Can these bones live?" (37:3). Often when we face the death of a loved one, we wonder how we will live without him or her. During a sacred conversation with a woman I ministered to on her deathbed, she wondered out loud how her loved ones would live without her. She was the central figurehead in the family. Death causes us to question how life will be different after death has touched us.

Dreams and visions have a way of entering our lives at the time of death. My grandmother heard my grandfather's voice the night after he died, and saw him get up out of bed to leave the room. What do such visions communicate? Can loved ones be immortalized in our dreams? Ezekiel answers this way, "O Lord God, you know" (37:3).

Prayer: God of the valley of the shadow of death, we confess our fear of the unknown. Let us trust in the knowledge that when our lives are touched by death your love will surround us. May our dreams bring us closer to those we love and to you. Amen.

Undead Dreams

Read Ezekiel 37:7–14.

So I prophesied as I had been commanded; and as I prophesied, suddenly there was a noise, a rattling, and the bones came together, bone to its bone. (Ezekiel 37:7)

Dreams have the power to raise the dead. This is a message threaded throughout scripture. We see it here in Ezekiel and we see it again in the life, death, and resurrection of Jesus Christ. Let us not be fooled—dreams are real. And dreams are what save us. Our dreamscape is where the impossible becomes possible, and new beginnings are born.

When we search our own hearts, what dreams do we find awaiting resurrection? Is there a dream lingering within your spirit that longs to have God breathe into it new life so that it may live? If that dream could resurrect itself, what would it look like manifesting before your eyes?

In the New Testament we hear about God's dream of a world grounded in the love of God. The gospel of Luke says that God's dream for us is simply this: "'Love the Lord your God with all your heart, and with all your soul, and with all your strength, and with all your mind; and your neighbor as yourself'" (Luke 10:27). How do your dreams lead you to more loving relationships with God, your neighbors, and yourself?

Prayer: God of undead dreams, we pray for the places in the world where sorrow and violence threaten to silence the dreamers. For communities facing systemic injustice, poverty, and oppression, we pray for you to raise up leaders, dreamers, and visionaries to help bring about renewal. Help us to create a world where streets are safe and where neighbors treat one another with love. Amen.

A Vision of Protection and Assurance

Read Genesis 15:1–3.

After these things the word of the LORD came to Abram in a vision, "Do not be afraid, Abram, I am your shield; your reward shall be very great." (Genesis 15:1)

The Hebrew word for vision is *chazah*, which means to see or behold. Genesis describes a time when Abram acknowledged that even if he had all the riches of the world, they would not be worth the one thing he wanted most: for his wife, Sarai, to bear a son. Even though Abram was successful in the public realm, in his own family life he felt like a failure.

Abram's spirit is distressed and hopeless, yet he remains faithful to his promise to God. In response to Abram's faithfulness, God appears to him in a vision, granting words of protection and assurance. God assures Abram that his "reward shall be very great" (15:1). Earlier, God called him to "go from your country, your people, and your father's household to the land I will show you" (12:1, NIV). This vision appears to Abram just in time, as fear had begun to creep into his mind.

This particular vision from God is a very personal one, directed at protecting Abram's well-being and giving him confidence as he seeks to do God's will. As one of the great leaders of the Hebrew people, the mental, physical, and spiritual health and wholeness of Abram matter. In order for him to lead effectively, Abram needs to remain grounded in God's word. Personal encounters with God give us strength for the journey, assuring us that no matter what challenges await, God is with us.

Prayer: God, like a shield, offer us your protection from anything that might harm us—body, mind and spirit. Help us to behold you, and to be assured of your love. Amen.

God's Dream of Infinity

Read Genesis 15:4–6.

He brought him outside and said, "Look toward heaven and count the stars, if you are able to count them." (Genesis 15:5)

God is a God of big dreams. Our spiritual inheritance is extraordinarily generous. Abram had no idea of the scope of God's dream for him and his people. The blessings that awaited him were more than the stars—too many to count.

Stargazing on a clear night invites us to contemplate the way of dreams and visions. Do you remember a time when your evening view of the heavens was unobstructed by artificial light? During one of my adventures as a youth traveling in Ireland, I met a local astronomer named Peter who traveled throughout the country with a telescope, giving seminars to schoolchildren. His dream was to meet and marry a woman who owned a hill. I couldn't help him fulfill that particular dream. But I could appreciate how studying the stars opens up our imagination and invites a deeper sense of wonder.

Abram didn't have a telescope like my Irish friend Peter to help him count the stars, nor, like us, did he have Google Sky on the Internet to gaze deeply into the heavens. But when God took Abram outside and told him the sky's the limit, Abram knew that God's dream of infinity was for real. Schedule a date night with God this week to gaze into the night sky and see what dreams appear.

Prayer: God of infinity, we praise you for the stars that remind us of the countless blessings we receive through the ages. Thank you for signs and wonders in the night sky that inspire us to dream big dreams. Amen.

Bad Dreams

Read Genesis 15:12–16.

As the sun was going down, a deep sleep fell upon Abram, and a deep and terrifying darkness descended upon him. (Genesis 15:12)

There's no good way to deliver bad news. Business coaches suggest that the best way to deliver bad news is fast. God chooses to break the bad news to Abram while he is in a "deep sleep." Is this a nightmare or a dream? While in this "terrifying darkness" Abram learns that the Israelites will be enslaved for 400 years and that only after four generations of oppression will they be reunited with their homeland. Abram gets no explanation from God as to why the excruciatingly long period of exile into slavery. In this dream encounter with God, Abram receives forewarning about the terror and tragedy that are to come to his people—and it is very bad news.

One of the most challenging religious questions of all-time, famously explored in the book of Job, as well as by Jewish scholars Elie Wiesel and Rabbi Harold Kushner, is "Why do bad things happen to good people?" God doesn't explain why in this passage. God simply tells Abram that things are going to get bad, very bad, before they get better.

When we wake up from a bad dream, it can be hard to shake it off. What if instead of wishing bad dreams away, we paid close attention to them and asked the question: Where is God in this bad dream? In Abram's case, God was present in the bad dream in the promise that things would get better. One day the Israelites would be free.

Prayer: God of the darkness, help us to see you even in the midst of bad dreams. Amen.

Abram's Night Vision of God's Covenant

Read Genesis 15:17–20.

When the sun had gone down and it was dark, a smoking fire pot and a flaming torch passed between these pieces. On that day the Lord *made a covenant with Abram, saying, "To your descendants I give this land..." (Genesis 15:17–19)*

Fire is a symbol that appears in the Bible as representative of God's presence, as seen here and in the famous text about Moses and the burning bush (Exodus 3:1–2). This vision of fire also signifies a ritual of sealing a contract that was common in Hebrew culture. Abram receives this vision in the dark on behalf of the nation of Israel. This text illuminates the sacredness of night visions.

Transformative leadership means submitting your life to God and allowing God to use you for the greater good. Abram's humility and faithfulness as a transformative leader allowed God's message to flow through him, without interference or distraction, to the people. What does such transformative leadership look like today? Whom do you entrust to receive God's contract on behalf of the people? How are our religious leaders engaged in covenant relationships and held accountable to God and to the community of faith?

Prayer: God of holy fire, thank you for transformative leaders who stand watch over the fire pots of your promise. Bless those holding vigil for us in the darkness of night. Amen.

Infertility, Desperation, and Dreams Derailed

Read Genesis 16:1–6.

Now Sarai, Abram's wife, bore him no children. She had an Egyptian slave-girl whose name was Hagar, and Sarai said to Abram, "You see that the LORD has prevented me from bearing children; go in to my slave-girl; it may be that I shall obtain children by her." (Genesis 16:1–2)

Sarai and Abram's dream of having children was seriously jeopardized by one thing: Sarai believed that God had closed her womb. Infertility was interpreted differently back then, before science and technology. So Sarai came up with her own way of fulfilling this dream: Use her slave woman's womb. This is a low point for Abram's wife, who abuses Hagar both by using her in this way, and in her ill treatment of Hagar once she is with child. Sarai acts out of desperation and lack of faith in God's ability to fulfill her vision of a family.

Like many of us, Sarai was anxious about God's timing. She was tired of waiting. It was her lack of faith that derailed God's dream. Instead of trusting that God would bless them with children, in time, Sarai took matters into her own hands, a decision she quickly regretted.

Today life seems extra complicated. There can be overwhelming obstacles interfering with our dreams and visions being realized. What happens when it seems as if the very thing we want most in the world, the thing we pray most fervently for, is out of reach, seemingly forever? Was there a time when you interfered in a situation to fix a problem that, it turns out, didn't need fixing?

Prayer: God of pregnant hopes, help us to wait patiently for dreams to be born when they are ready. Help us to trust your timing. Amen.

Exiles and Visions of Freedom

Read Genesis 16:7–10.

The angel of the LORD found her by a spring of water in the wilderness…
And he said, "Hagar, slave-girl of Sarai, where have you come from and
where are you going?" (Genesis 16:7–8)

After running away from her master Sarai, pregnant Hagar stops
to rest beside a spring of water in the wilderness. Hagar experiences
a vision of an angel of God who calls her by name. Since the angel
knows Hagar's name and that she is the slave of Sarai, why does the
angel continue asking Hagar where she has come from and where
she is going? Does the angel know something about Hagar that she
herself does not yet know?

Hagar ran away because she wanted to be free. Yet the angel
directs her to return to Sarai and Abram, and then promises to
bless her descendants. What is the angel thinking? Hagar fled
seeking safety because of the danger of Sarai's abuse. Escaping an
unsafe environment, Hagar chooses to struggle for survival alone
in the wilderness while she is pregnant rather than to be a slave. It
is disturbing that Hagar's vision of freedom is interrupted by the
angel's directions to return and be submissive to Sarai.

Biblical passages that speak to the master-slave relationship
recall times throughout history when our ancestors have been
masters, slaves, or exiles. We cannot ignore the disturbing realities of
power used to oppress people in the Bible and in today's world (in
the form of human trafficking, for example). We could even pose the
very question the angel asks Hagar and apply it to our own history
of slavery, racism, and oppression created by systemic inequalities:
"Where have you come from and where are you going?" How has
our history shaped our understanding of what it means to be free,
to be equal, and to be a citizen? Where do we need to go if things
are to change?

Prayer: God of the slave and the exile, strengthen us for the long walk home
to freedom. Amen.

In God's Eyes

Read Genesis 16:11–16.

So she named the LORD who spoke to her, "You are El-roi"; for she said, "Have I really seen God and remained alive after seeing him?" (Genesis 16:13)

Eyes are the window to the soul. Think of a time when you noticed the eyes of someone you love. Before my son started walking, I often carried him outside so he could look up at the sky. I'll never forget the time when, holding him close, I saw the sky reflected in his eyes. In that fleeting moment, all at once I saw a glimpse of his soul as well as a window to heaven. I saw God.

Hagar's encounter with God is a window into God's soul. She sees God seeing her. It's a moment of profound contact, a moment of opening, a moment of deep connection with the divine. Hagar's experience with God affirms her identity as a woman of God, challenging the labels of society: slave, mistress, and foreigner. In God's eyes, Hagar is worthy of blessings.

Like many of us, Hagar questions this encounter with God before it's even finished. Did that really just happen to me? God is visible to those who have eyes to see. And if you are looking for God, don't be surprised if you discover God looking back at you, as a mother tenderly gazes upon a child in her arms. When we look upon others with eyes of blessings, we can, without words, show God's love.

Prayer: Thank you God for noticing us, for seeing us, even when we question the power of your presence in our lives. Help us to see others with eyes of love. Amen.

Hagar's Desert Dream

Read Genesis 21:8–18.

And God heard the voice of the boy; and the angel of God called to Hagar from heaven, and said to her, "What troubles you, Hagar? Do not be afraid; for God has heard the voice of the boy where he is. Come, lift up the boy and hold him fast with your hand, for I will make a great nation of him." (Genesis 21:17–18)

Sarah is so disturbed and threatened by Hagar and her son Ishmael that she demands they both be banished from her sight. I can barely stand to read the rest of this story, it is so awful. Yet even in the midst of this heartbreaking saga, we see the timeless characteristic of God demonstrated: God honors promises. When God promises Abraham that Hagar's son will be blessed, God follows through, ensuring the survival of Hagar and Ishmael.

In the wilderness, a dry desert land, Hagar runs out of water, which is certain to lead to death. Tragically she feels she has no choice but to abandon her son under a bush. The scripture says that once Hagar is far away from her son, she bursts into tears. Swiftly God responds to the cries of the child left behind and God instructs Hagar to follow the plans God has for them. Here God demonstrates faithfulness to fulfill the promises that God made, "I will make a great nation of him."

How many of us have found ourselves in situations where all seems lost? Like Hagar we often abandon the gifts God has given us because we simply cannot see a way forward. Even in this time of crisis, encounters with God's angels and dreams in the desert open our eyes to new ways forward, possibilities for life even in the face of death. Just when it seems our dreams are near death, God creates a way for resurrection.

Prayer: God of near death experiences, help us to dare to dream in the desert, and to see a new way forward. Resurrect the child within us that longs to live out our dreams. Amen.

God Helps Mothers to See

Read: Genesis 21:19–21.

Then God opened her eyes and she saw a well of water. So she went and filled the skin with water and gave the boy a drink (Genesis 21:19, NIV).

If we want to faithfully respond to God's Spirit moving in our lives, we first need to pay attention to the Spirit. The scripture says that Hagar's eyes were closed so she couldn't see what God was providing for her. God showed up in the dry desert and provided Hagar a well of water, but at first she couldn't see it because her eyes were closed.

Hagar's eyes were closed because her heart was ripped apart: She failed at caring for the child she birthed. Shrouded in grief and despair, she could not see any sign of life. The scripture says that "God opened her eyes." When mothers in the desert open their eyes and see water, the first thing they do is share that water with their children. International relief organizations know that when women have resources, communities are nurtured because women are more likely to share what they have to improve the lives of their children and those in need.

If God were to open your eyes and show you a well of water, to whom would you give water? If the mothers in your community could see resources available to help them and their children, what would that look like? How might God be calling your church to help mothers care better for their children?

Prayer: Show us how our congregation can provide "wells of water" for mothers who are looking for resources to care for their families in need. Amen.

Spiritual Energy under Fire

Read 1 Samuel 1:4–20

Hannah was praying silently; only her lips moved, but her voice was not heard; therefore Eli thought she was drunk. (1 Samuel 1:13 NRSV)

Childless for years, Hannah went to pray in the temple, passionately asking God to bless her and her husband with a son. She was a sight to behold: weeping, rocking, wringing her hands, and moving her lips without sound. When the temple priest Eli looked upon her, he surmised that Hannah's infertility had driven her to alcoholism, so that she couldn't even come to temple sober. Immediately Eli judged Hannah, accusing her of dishonoring the temple, and stood on the verge of kicking her out. What Eli couldn't see is that God's Spirit, not alcohol, stirred within her.

Hannah exhibited electrifying spiritual energy that was visible to Eli, but he didn't understand its source. Possibly he had never seen someone praying so hard for something that it resembled drunken behavior. Did Hannah pray more feverishly than he ever had, even though he himself was a priest?

How easy it can be for us to gaze upon others with suspicion when they exhibit great passion in prayer and worship. We see out of the corner of our eye someone engaging their fully body and a discomfort may arise within us. How often do we allow ourselves to be drunk with the spiritual energy harnessed by focused, earnest prayer for the deepest desires of our heart? Hannah's spirituality is an example of ancient biblical mysticism, where she is so acutely attuned to God's Spirit that it causes others to be uncomfortable and question her grounding in reality.

Prayer: God of spiritual fire, grant us passion in our prayer life. Help us to be fully engaged in body, mind and spirit during our conversations with you. Amen.

Hannah's Vision of Justice

Read 1 Samuel 2:1–10.

The LORD makes poor and makes rich;
*   he brings low, he also exalts.*
He raises up the poor from the dust;
*   he lifts the needy from the ash heap,*
to make them sit with princes
*   and inherit a seat of honor.*
For the pillars of the earth are the LORD's,
*   and on them he has set the world. (1 Samuel 2:7–8)*

The Bible contains several strong women of faith, including Hannah, who fiercely prayed for a son. God fulfilled the desire of Hannah's heart, and she gave birth to a son she named Samuel. As promised, Hannah dedicated her son to the service of God, raising him to become a priest, giving him to God. Hannah offers a prayer and vision for her son as she entrusts him to the care of the temple priest Eli. In her prayer emerges a vision of God's justice.

Weapons of mass destruction will be broken, the oversized will be downsized, and those who are thrown into the garbage will be sitting in places of honor. Hannah envisions a world where greatness is not measured by wealth or military might, but by acts of kindness and mercy. And it is to this vision that Hannah entrusts her son.

What kind of world do we envision our daughters and sons to help shape? What role can our children play in creating peaceful relationships, developing just practices, and treating the earth and its creatures with kindness? What if we, like Hanna, were to entrust the young with God's vision of justice?

Prayer: We pray for the children and youth of the world. Help us to make room for them to shape the church, leading us toward justice. Amen.

Eve's Vision of Wisdom

Read Genesis 3:1–8.

So when the woman saw that the tree was good for food, and that it was a delight to the eyes, and that the tree was to be desired to make one wise, she took of its fruit and ate; and she also gave some to her husband, who was with her, and he ate. (Genesis 3:6)

The first woman mentioned in the Bible is Eve, of course. We get a sense of her powerful intellect in this passage, where she is hungry not only for food but also for knowledge. Yet this is not just any type of information, like the weather forecast—this is the information at the heart of wisdom: the knowledge of good and evil.

Eve possessed a special kind of vision that allowed her to see beyond the normal surface of the garden. She could see the wisdom hanging from the tree's branches. In fact, Eve was the one who first encountered the talking serpent; Adam didn't seem to have a clue about what was going on in the garden. When Eve offered Adam the fruit, he ate it without question. Was this all a dream?

The desire to share wisdom is demonstrated by Eve's actions when she gives some of the fruit to Adam. I believe Eve's intentions are pure in this exchange. If anything, it is the serpent who first questioned God's warning about eating the fruit in the middle of the garden. Eve wanted to follow God's instruction, but the vision of wisdom before her and the temptation was too powerful.

Not all visions and dreams are good for us to act on. It's important to have trusted people in your life who can help you discern what is from God and what just might be from a serpent in the garden.

Prayer: We pray for discernment when unhealthy visions appear before us, tempting us to disobey God's loving instructions that keep us safe. Amen.

Dream Interrupted

Read Genesis 3:9–24.

Then the LORD God said to the woman, "What is this that you have done" The woman said, "The serpent tricked me, and I ate." (Genesis 3:13)

The garden was God's dreamland. Created to be a place of beauty, play, joy, and delight, the garden was the first home of our spiritual mother and father. It was God's dream that Adam and Eve live in the garden, surrounded by everything they would ever need or want—everything except for knowledge of good and evil, and immortality. And this is where God's dream is deferred.

In what appears to be an unexpected twist, catching God by surprise, God catches Eve and Adam right after they've digested the fruit—the seeds of the fruit wet on the ground at their feet. Because God never intended to create demigods, that is, immortal beings that know everything that God knows, Adam and Eve are banished from the garden.

God's dream is interrupted by unforeseen circumstances. If even God didn't predict the serpent would come and ruin things, then surely we mere mortals will have our dreams interrupted again and again. Things will happen that we didn't see coming. Serpents will interfere with our plans, interrupting our dreams, even killing them. People get tricked and people get escorted out of the garden. Each day is a resurrection of God's dream, a chance to get it right and enjoy the simple pleasures of life in the garden.

Prayer: When situations arise that are outside my control, help me to patiently pursue God's dream for my life, knowing that even God's dream gets interrupted sometimes. Amen.

Miriam's Victory Dance

Read Exodus 15:1–21.

Then the prophet Miriam, Aaron's sister, took a tambourine in her hand; and all the women went out after her with tambourines and with dancing. (Exodus 15:20)

The people of Israel were led by Moses and his sister Miriam out of slavery and into freedom. As a prophet, Miriam inspired people to follow her because God blessed her with a vision of victory. Miriam saw the angel of God traveling with them. She knew that God was present in the clouds that covered the Egyptian armies at night and that God was present in the wind that blew the sea back, revealing dry ground for the Israelites to cross over to freedom.

Miriam's ability to envision victory keeps her focused on fulfilling God's dream of freedom, even when her people cry out in despair because the road to freedom is filled with fear and near death experiences. The first thing Miriam does when her people arrive safely across the Red Sea is to lead all the women in praising God for their victory. They must have been exhausted, but they were not too tired to dance and give thanks to God.

Especially when the struggle is long and people are weary, it is crucial for leaders to remain focused on the vision of victory. With an eye on the prize, a sighting of God's presence along the way provides much needed encouragement. What vision has God placed upon your community for victory? How is this vision of victory lifted up? What are some signs that God is with you?

Prayer: We thank you, God, for leaders like Miriam who hold fast to the vision of victory. Help us to be like Miriam and to rejoice in your power to save us. Amen.

Dreaming Up the Ladder

Read Genesis 28:10–22.

And he (Jacob) dreamed that there was a ladder set up on the earth, the top of it reaching to heaven; and the angels of God were ascending and descending on it. (Genesis 28:12)

As people of faith we trust that God is at work in our lives. What is also true is that God calls each of us to fully embrace the blessings of heaven, right here and right now. Jacob's dream is a beautiful illustration of how angels travel up and down the ladder, to and from heaven, to bring blessings down to earth from above. God's message is clear: I will bless you wherever you go; I will not leave you.

The dreams and visions in the Bible, I am convinced, are there to show us how real and how close God is to us. It's time to lie still, with our ears to the ground, so that we can hear the angels coming, delivering to earth blessings from heaven. Take a moment to consider which area of your life (family, church, community) is in need of blessings from above.

One way to think about prayer is to picture ourselves lying at the base of Jacob's ladder. Prayer is waiting on God to deliver on the promise to bless us and to be with us for the journey ahead. In our prayers we dare to imagine our dreams fulfilled, and our hearts open to trusting God's word.

Prayer: Help us to look heavenward next time we are tempted to think the ladder is not meant for us or our dreams. Give us faith, like Jacob, to believe in your goodness. Amen.

When Dreams Divide

Read Genesis 37:1–11.

Once Joseph had a dream, and when he told it to his brothers, they hated him even more. He said to them, "Listen to this dream that I dreamed." (Genesis 37:5–6)

Sometimes dreams get us in trouble. Joseph is a dreamer; he cannot help it. Joseph doesn't keep his dreams secret, but shares them with his brothers, and eventually with his father. Each time Joseph tells his dream, the divide between him and his family grows. The scripture says that they "hated him even more" after hearing the dream.

When we get mixed messages, understanding one thing from God and hearing something else from our family, it puts us in a difficult spot. Joseph chooses to trust God's dreams, even when doing so causes division within his family. This dynamic is familiar to me, as I've listened to the struggles of people to answer a call to ministry, whether in a traditional church or ministry in alternative settings. For my gay, lesbian, bisexual, transgender, and questioning Christian sisters and brothers, living into God's dream for their lives is often divisive. Not all branches of the Christian family tree have embraced and celebrate their ministry. Yet, faithful to God's dream, they seek ministry partners and affirmation elsewhere.

Joseph's dream dynamic reminds us that sometimes dreams cause disturbances in the family system, in the church, and in the world. This resistance need not prevent us from pursuing God's dream for our lives. What impresses me about Joseph is that he doesn't let his brothers' hatred stop him from living into his dreams. Known locally as "the dreamer," Joseph's identity is defined by his relationship with God, not by his dependence on other people approving of him. Christians often don't like to upset people. But maybe, like Joseph, when it's a cause worth supporting, it's okay to be unpopular.

Prayer: When there is hatred and division, help us to focus more fiercely on our dreams, trusting that in the end our dreams will lead us to an unseen wholeness. Amen.

Seeking Spiritual Direction

Read Genesis 40:1–23.

They said to him, "We have had dreams, and there is no one to interpret them." And Joseph said to them, "Do not interpretations belong to God? Please tell them to me." (Genesis 40:8)

Influential leaders inspire us by their ability to cast a vision. They make it seem so easy, as if they suddenly woke up one morning and had an epiphany. The truth is, for discerning leaders in complicated times, going it alone is very dangerous. Transformative leadership is not a solo act. The healthiest leaders seek insight and support from trusted peers, mentors, counselors, and spiritual directors.

In this text Joseph serves as a spiritual director/dream interpreter for the chief baker and cupbearer. Joseph tells them what the dreams mean for their lives. That the chief cupbearer then forgets about Joseph after his life is spared illustrates an attitude that exists today toward mental health care. We undervalue those who can help us see deeper truths emerging from our minds, even when they save our lives. The shame and stigma surrounding brain health prohibits us from being truly healthy. We very rarely talk about mental illness in church, with few exceptions, and our clergy usually prefer not to preach about it.

In some deeper sense, Joseph was a mental health counselor, guiding others in the navigation of their minds' dreams. The question posed by the chief cupbearer and baker is an important one for all of us to ponder, and perhaps even spend time with a mental health counselor to explore how we might interpret our dreams. Mental health is not only about correcting brain functions when there is a disease such as anxiety or depression, but also about creating the best case scenario for our brains to function. The brain is an important part of our physical health. Paying attention to our dreams leads to healthier brains and lives.

Prayer: We give thanks for spiritual directors, counselors, and therapists who listen to our dreams and help us find deeper meaning and mental and spiritual health. Amen.

Witnessing Wisdom

Read Genesis 41:1–40.

"Since God has shown you all this, there is no one so discerning and wise as you." (Genesis 41:39)

Spiritual discernment is the daily work of the Christian life. Discernment often happens through a series of questions. Where is God showing up? Where is my spirit being drawn? How is my spirit fed? Whom do I trust with my heart? Spending time with these questions may stir within us a response to God's dream for our lives.

Part of what made Joseph a gifted dream interpreter was his ability to discern how God was present in the dream. Wisdom guided Joseph to know what to say to Pharaoh. God's wisdom comes to us through a relationship with God. Discernment depends on accessing divine wisdom, through valuing the connections we have with the earth, with spiritual teachers, and with ourselves.

It is up to us how we will use our gifts of discernment and wisdom. Will our dreams and visions benefit the earth? The biblical witness reminds us that God uses human dreams to fulfill divine purpose in the world. What may seem like a personal dream very well might have the potential to transform a family, community, or society. One of the roles of faith communities is to discern who the dreamers and visionaries are in society and connect them to the building of God's realm on earth as it is in heaven.

Prayer: Show us wisdom and discernment as we engage with the world so that we harness the dreams and visions that will save us all. Amen.

God Is Still Speaking

Read Genesis 46:1–7.

God spoke to Israel in visions of the night, and said, "Jacob, Jacob." And he said, "Here I am." (Genesis 46:2)

Open up your Bible to the Table of Contents and you will typically find the books of the Bible divided into two main sections labeled "The Old Testament" and "The New Testament." Preacher and educator Bishop Yvette Flunder argues that it is time for a "Third Testament" that gives an updated perspective about how the people of God have evolved in the twenty-first century with regard to human sexuality. Indeed, with the changes recently made in the laws of government and in the laws of most mainline Christian denominations, public views and understandings of sexuality and identity have radically changed over the past decades.

Considering an addition to the Christian canon is not a new idea, though it remains controversial. However, as we see in today's text, one of the consistent characteristics of God in the scripture and in the witness of the church throughout time is that God is still speaking. God continues to communicate with us, just as God spoke to Jacob in the night vision. Were God's words more important in the past than they are now? Did God speak with greater authority to our ancestors? Are we listening to what God says in the night?

In this exchange between God and Jacob, we overhear Jacob's response to God, "Here I am." God calls in the night, in our visions, and we respond, "here we are." This is how to make bold and courageous moves. Whether it's expanding the biblical witness to include a testimony that proclaims everyone is welcome in God's family, or communicating the radical love of God that black lives matter—we must listen expectantly in the night, attuned to God's voice.

Prayer: God of night visions, help us to incline our ear to the sound of your voice, entrusting ourselves to your call upon our lives. Amen.

Intergenerational Visions

Read Genesis 48:1–11.

Israel said to Joseph, "I did not expect to see your face; and here God has let me see your children also." (Genesis 48:11)

The sandwich generation finds themselves with generations both behind (aging parents) and ahead (maturing children) of them needing their attention, resources, and time. To be in this position of caregiver for multiple generations is often exhausting and stressful, creating pressure to provide support that is beyond healthy limits. One of the advantages of multigenerational relationships is the opportunity to learn from the stories and experiences that cross the span of time.

This multigenerational dynamic appears in the family of Joseph when he takes his two sons to see their dying grandfather Jacob. During their visit Jacob tells his son and grandsons about an old vision he had when "God Almighty (El-Shaddai) appeared to me at Luz in the land of Canaan, and he blessed me, and said to me, 'I am going to make you fruitful and increase your numbers'" (Genesis 48:3–4). In this visit with their grandfather, Joseph's sons hear about a vision of God appearing and speaking words of incredible blessing. This vision of God was to have tremendous impact on their lives, and before he died Jacob was able to share it with his grandsons.

Congregations are ripe for creating opportunities for intergenerational conversations about dreams and visions. Such sharing opens our eyes to see God in new ways. Like Joseph and Jacob, we can come beside one another with our children, and listen to the stories of God showing up and blessing us.

Prayer: God Almighty, help us to spend time hearing the stories of all ages, so that the blessings you pour out on one generation can be shared with the next. Amen.

The Test

Read Genesis 49:22–28.

Blessings of the skies above,
  blessings of the deep springs below,
  blessings of the breast and womb.
Your father's blessings are greater
  than the blessings of the ancient mountains,
  than the bounty of the age-old hills. (Genesis 49:25–26, NIV)

Jacob's journey portrayed in the Bible teaches us that one of the ways we know that dreams and visions are from God is if they bring blessings. So to test whether or not a dream or vision is from God is to see how it reflects the promised blessings of God. In the scripture passage for today we see that blessings of the skies, the springs, the milk of the breast, and the amniotic fluid of the womb all flow from Jacob's relationship with dreams. This is how he knows his dreams and visions are from God: Blessings pour out from them.

Testing our dreams and visions is a spiritual discipline. The testing phase begins as soon as the dream or vision is manifested, and continues as understanding unfolds about the implications of the dream or vision. For example, a youth minister dreams of starting a new program at the church for housing insecure LGBTQ teenagers. Questions to test this dream include: Does it bless those receiving services? Does it bless the church? Does it bless the volunteers? Does it bless the community? Does it glorify God? Once there is clarity that the dream is from God, then steps can be taken to communicate the dream among members in the community to see if there is support for moving forward.

Prayer: Not all dreams and visions are from you, God of blessings. Grant us wisdom and discernment as we seek to understand our dreams and visions so that we know which ones are from you. Amen.

Vision Evangelism

Read Habakkuk 2:1–3.

Then the LORD *answered me and said:*
Write the vision;
  make it plain on tablets,
  so that a runner may read it. (Habakkuk 2:2)

The entire book of Habakkuk is considered an oracle or a vision that came to the prophet from God. The verse for today's focus explains how the prophet came to author this text: God told him to do so. Translated into today's terms, the verse might read this way: Then the LORD answered me and said: "Tweet the vision; type it in 140 characters, so that it may be retweeted." Social media is the fastest growing form of evangelism in the world. The good news of the gospel can be transmitted through websites, Facebook, Twitter, Instagram, and blogs. Obviously, tablets are passé, so we use the communication tools of our age to do what God tells the biblical prophet to do: Write the vision and make it plain.

Paul Raushenbush, editor of Global Spirituality and Religion for the online news source Huffington Post, says the church needs to find ways to speak to new generations whose primary source of information (and community) is found online. Today whenever there is a question, the first place people look for an answer is Google. Is my baby's rash serious? Will my dog need surgery? Is there a coffee shop nearby? When people have questions about God, they take them to Google. Is heaven real? Is homosexuality a sin?

There is a radical vision of God's love that includes everyone, regardless of religion, age, race, politics, mental and physical ability, sexual orientation, gender or identity. Is this vision written plainly on the Internet so that people may read it?

Prayer: God of the prophets, give us courage to write your vision, make it plain, and share it with the world so that all may hear the good news of your love. Amen.

Old Dreamers, Young Visionaries

Read Joel 2:28–32.

Then afterward
I will pour out my spirit on all flesh;
your sons and your daughters shall prophesy,
your old men shall dream dreams,
and your young men shall see visions. (Joel 2:28)

In the immediate aftermath of the terrorist attacks of September 11, 2001, the United States witnessed the world responding with a generous outpouring of compassion and mercy. There was an outpouring of God's Spirit. We heard courageous Christian voices call out for peace, rejecting war as the answer. In the face of knee-jerk discrimination toward all Muslims and the burning of the Koran, we heard Christian leaders share dreams and visions of interfaith dialogue and cooperation.

The prophet Joel's words are born from a devastating disaster experienced by his people: an army of locusts creating a desert wasteland where there was once the Garden of Eden. God's response to tragedy is to show up in the prophesies, dreams, and visions of the people. Like applying aloe onto sunburned skin, God's Spirit is poured out "on all flesh" in the aftermath. When things hurt the most and we are feeling burned, God is there to soothe and comfort us. This is incarnation: God in the flesh, through the power of God's Spirit.

The way forward after the 9/11 attack (or the locust attack) is to listen to the prophets, dreamers, and visionaries. Too often these voices our drowned out by political leaders and media messages tainted with greed, vengeance, and a disregard for an ethic of reconciliation. Communities of faith nurture this prophetic witness of dreamers and visionaries so that when the time comes, the church can witness to love in the world. Old and young, male and female, God's Spirit is poured out "on all flesh." It's the work of the church to lift up these voices so that God's vision and dream for the world may be known.

Prayer: We gratefully receive the outpouring of your Spirit, God, and devote ourselves to nurturing the prophets, dreamers and visionaries among us. Amen.

Vision Is More Than a Statement

Read Proverbs 29:1–27.

Where there is no vision, the people perish. (Proverbs 29:18, SGL)

Do you know your church's mission and vision statement? Does your church have such statements? In the past few decades, congregations have begun to pay closer attention to prioritizing their time and resources on what matters most. Mission and vision statements concentrate the greatest hopes and dreams we have for our identity as the Body of Christ. The mission statement states concisely the work that matters most to us, and the vision statement states why it matters.

Do followers of Christ know why it matters to be Christian? Do we have a clear vision of why it matters that we follow the way of Jesus? "When there is no vision, the people perish," says the author of Proverbs. Vision is more than a statement; vision is a lived understanding of our calling to give our lives to Christ. If we have a vision from God, it is because God has made a home within our hearts. In this case, it's got to be all or nothing—lukewarm Christianity is perishing, the churches and people along with it.

Now is the time for new visions. A new vision is better than no vision, so what is there to fear? When death is how the story ends, it's time to write the next chapter, a chapter where the Crucified Christ is glorified and raised from the dead.

Prayer: God of vitality and energy, show us a new vision that will lead us to new life. Amen.

God's Search Committee

Read Psalm 89:9–29.

Then you spoke in a vision to your faithful one, and said:
  "I have set the crown on one who is mighty,
  I have exalted one chosen from the people." (Psalm 89:19)

When people are asked why they choose to attend a particular congregation for worship, often they cite one of these three aspects: people, preaching, and music. Congregations that don't have all three struggle. When a congregation loses good people, a minister, or the music director, things can feel unsettled. The time of rebuilding good people, good preaching, and good music is critical to the health of the church.

Pastoral search committees will often pray for God to show them a vision of who is going to be the best woman or man for the position. Often the answer is unexpected. One church was certain that its next pastor was going to be a forty-something white man with a stay-at-home wife and two young children. Yet after months of work and prayer, the top candidate was a childless woman who was in a same-gender loving relationship. The one for whom the crown was set and exalted was not who they expected. After intentional conversations with the congregation about why this was the best candidate, the church voted unanimously to call the new pastor— truly the work of the Spirit.

Without vision, we will not find our way into the realm of God. We limit God's ability to transform us and we limit our imagination when we close our eyes to seeing God's vision for us. Whether it is the work of a pastoral search committee, a transition in your personal life, or some other occasion for change, intentionally seeking God's vision grants us peace of mind knowing that we are indeed doing God's will.

Prayer: We pray for all ministers who are in search of a call; may they and the search committees be led by God's vision. Amen.

Prophetic Visions and Dreams

Read Numbers 12:1–16.

And he said, "Hear my words:
When there are prophets among you,
I the LORD make myself known to them in visions;
I speak to them in dreams." (Numbers 12:6)

It's happened to all of us. We whisper under our breath a criticism about someone else in the room and somehow we are overheard by an unintended listener. Miriam and Aaron were in the same embarrassing situation. They commented with disapproval on Moses' choice in marrying a foreign woman. This time it's God who is eavesdropping. God defends Moses as the only human on earth that speaks to God face to face. God punishes Miriam (and not Aaron, strangely enough) by cursing her with leprosy, and expels her outside of camp for a week. Harsh.

This story gives us a glimpse into how the Hebrew people understood communication with God. Unless you were Moses, God didn't speak to you directly, but indirectly through the visions and dreams of the prophets. Miriam is one of those prophets whom God spoke through in a vision of freedom. Yet even prophets can make mistakes and incur the wrath of God.

This passage says in Numbers 12:8 that unlike direct and clear face-to-face communication with God, visions and dreams come in the form of riddles. A riddle requires work to understand it because its meaning is hidden. Riddles draw us deeper in thought and demand that we invest ourselves in finding the answer. This is a helpful framework for thinking about a life of faith. It is most often clouded with uncertainty and questions, like a vision or dream itself. If God intends it to be this way, then what is to be learned by entering into the cloud, rather than turning away?

Prayer: God of riddles, draw us more deeply into the cloud of unknowing, so that we may discover truth in the questions. Amen.

Mysteries of Heaven

Read Daniel 2:1–23.

Then the mystery was revealed to Daniel in a vision of the night, and Daniel blessed the God of heaven. (Daniel 2:19)

King Nebuchadnezzar was losing sleep. The scripture says that he couldn't sleep because his mind was troubled. Was he suffering from anxiety, depression, or obsessive compulsive disorder? The King said his dreams troubled him, so he sought out the experts of that age: magicians, enchanters, sorcerers, and astrologers (today's Jungian analysts, therapists, and psychologists). But none of these experts could help him. In a fit of rage he ordered all of the wise men of the region to be executed.

Daniel was among the wise men slated for execution. However, once Daniel heard about the king's troubles, Daniel knew that if he could meet the king, he could help him. This epiphany came to Daniel in a "vision of the night." Upon meeting the king, he explained that there was only One that was powerful enough to reveal to the king the mystery of his dream. Then Daniel began unfolding the mystery of the king's dream, and when he finished, the king proclaimed, "Truly your God is a God of gods and the Lord of kings and a revealer of mysteries, for you have been able to reveal this mystery" (Daniel 2:47).

Daniel is clear about the source of his gifts: the God of heaven. He gives God all of the credit and because of this, God's name is glorified and people come to believe in God. The spiritual gifts of Christians are nothing to be ashamed of or to hide, but rather are meant to be shared with the world, even with kings. Aware of the power of visions and dreams, Christians can engage with the world, looking for opportunities to unfold the mysteries of our time. The ability to interpret God's activity in the world is a gift.

Prayer: God of night visions, help us engage the mysteries of our age with open minds, ripe to receive and share your blessings from heaven. Amen.

Writing Down the Dream

Read Daniel 7:1–14.

In the first year of King Belshazzar of Babylon, Daniel had a dream and visions of his head as he lay in bed. Then he wrote down the dream. (Daniel 7:1)

We know Daniel the dream interpreter and how his mad skills landed him a job working for the King. Here we meet Daniel the dreamer and visionary when he makes his debut boldly envisioning an apocalypse like no other recorded in the Old Testament. A visionary, Daniel sees divine scenarios; seeing what others cannot see is what makes him a visionary.

Daniel writes down the dream. He does this because he does not yet understand its meaning. The act of writing itself is a spiritual discipline. Writing unfolds the mysteries of the vision. At the end of his written description of the apocalyptic vision, Daniel says, "This is the end of the matter. I, Daniel, was deeply troubled by my thoughts, and my face turned pale, but I kept the matter to myself" (Daniel 7:28, NIV). Writing also helps Daniel become aware of the mental toll these visions have on him physically. Even though Daniel chooses to keep this vision to himself, the act of writing his visions frees them from the chambers of his mind.

Try keeping a dream or vision journal. See if there are thoughts in your mind that would free you if you wrote them out. You don't need to share these writings with anyone. Pay close attention to what happens when you take the time to write down your dreams.

Prayer: God of revelation, help us see you more clearly in our dreams and visions. Amen.

Damascus Dream

Read Acts 9:1–19.

So Ananias went and entered the house. He laid his hands on Saul and said, "Brother Saul, the Lord Jesus, who appeared to you on your way here, has sent me so that you may regain your sight and be filled with the Holy Spirit." And immediately something like scales fell from his eyes, and his sight was restored. Then he got up and was baptized. (Acts 9:17–18)

The apostle Paul, formerly known as Saul, was baptized and changed his name in response to his encounter with the living Christ. Paul became a follower of The Way, the early name for Christians, because the Lord said, "he is an instrument whom I have chosen" (Acts 9:15). Paul's conversion demonstrates that God's grace and mercy are extended to all, despite our past and the damage we may have done to ourselves or to others. Paul's Damascus dream dramatically portrays the key role that visions play in the New Testament witness.

At the heart of Paul's Damascus dream is a vision of lightning flashing all around him, followed by hearing the voice of Jesus speaking directly to him (verses 3–5). Paul's traveling companions also heard this voice, but they could not see anything. Speechless, they led Paul, temporarily blind, into the city of Damascus. The Lord sent the disciple Ananias to go to Paul and usher him into discipleship.

One of the greatest mysteries of the Christian faith is how followers of The Way continue to experience the powerful presence of the Lord. Not everyone will have a Damascus Dream, but many do. Around the world, people are filled with the Holy Spirit and scales fall from their eyes, restoring their sight. And they are baptized into new life in Christ. Jesus Christ, as the son of God, offers us a unique way of seeing, dreaming, and experiencing God.

Prayer: Help us to hear your voice, Lord, in the lightning that interrupts our plans for mischief, replacing it with plans for building your realm. Amen.

Afternoon Tea with an Angel

Read Acts 10:1–8.

One afternoon at about three o'clock he had a vision in which he clearly saw an angel of God coming in and saying to him, "Cornelius." He stared at him in terror and said, "What is it, Lord?" He answered, "Your prayers and your alms have ascended as a memorial before God." (Acts 10:3–4)

A tradition originating in China centuries ago, drinking tea has many proven health benefits. In the mid-nineteenth century, the English popularized afternoon tea as a ritual between lunch and dinner. It is designed to be a thoughtful pause in the flow of time. Afternoon tea was a time for savoring a life of leisure, typically celebrated by upper class women. It was near tea time when the angel in Acts arrives as a surprise guest to Cornelius' home.

The scripture describes this afternoon tea with an angel as a "vision." In this vision the angel gives Cornelius instructions, telling him to find Peter and bring him back to Caesarea. Cornelius' first response to the angel is fear; he was not expecting the angel to visit him. Immediately the angel calms Cornelius by noting how his prayers and donations to the poor have honored God.

When our day is interrupted by unexpected guests, we can become suspicious, like Cornelius. Perhaps visions appear to us in the form of angels in disguise. God can use any of us as an instrument and God's presence can be felt at any time of day—in the night or at three in the afternoon. Cornelius asks the angel, "What is it, Lord?" This is the response of faith, to open ourselves up to what the Lord asks of us, especially when we are least prepared.

Prayer: Lord, in the beauty of afternoon light, when angels often surprise us, help us not to be resistant or afraid to respond. Amen.

Embodying a Vision

Read Acts 10:9–23.

Peter went up on the roof to pray...he fell into a trance. (Acts 10:9–10)

Peter's trance took him deep into a vision of heaven opening up, and what came down was a message of radical inclusion. After much thought, Peter realizes that the message of the vision was that everything God makes is good; there are no longer categories of pure and impure, clean and unclean. Peter says, "God does not show favoritism" (Acts 10:34, NIV).

In the early days of building the Jesus movement, it was a critical moment when Peter realized that the good news of peace through Jesus is universal. Somehow over time, the church today has forgotten what Peter learned from his vision. We still hear preachers, congregations, and church organizations being selective about who is included in God's realm. If it is true that God shows no favoritism, then why do Christians?

We don't need to fall into a trance on the rooftop in order to embody the vision that Peter is talking about (although, if you have a rooftop garden, it might not be a bad idea). As people of faith, as communities of faith, we can embody this radical message of inclusion by being intentional about who is sitting at the boardroom table, at the communion table, and at the kids' table. As the Body of Christ, what small but great thing can you start doing to show that all lives matter, not just the "pure" or "clean" ones?

Prayer: God of the clean and unclean, pure and impure, thank you for the vision to see that all are created in your image. Amen.

Visions of Mercy

Read Acts 16:6–15.

During the night Paul had a vision: there stood a man of Macedonia pleading with him and saying, "Come over to Macedonia and help us." (Acts 16:9)

Western Christianity exists because of a vision. Paul's vison of a man of Macedonia led him to travel across the sea, expanding the reach of the Christian message. The vision was a desperate invitation to come and help. From this vision Paul concluded that it was God's desire for him to preach the gospel in Macedonia. This is a vison of mercy.

Just outside the Macedonian city gates Paul meets a group of women sitting by the river. He and his companions intend to find a quiet place for prayer, but instead they encounter a group of women with whom they sit and begin a conversation. During this impromptu revival, the heart of a woman named Lydia is opened by the Lord, leading her and her entire household to be baptized. This is how Christianity spread, one conversation, one heart, one baptism at a time.

To think that it started with a vision of mercy. Ministry is a willingness to listen to an invitation and to respond when we are called to serve. Faith is not shared by force or coercion, and we cannot make new disciples by begging people to come to church. Like Paul, we need people who are willing to walk through the city streets, wander down by the riverside, and sit with the locals and talk.

Prayer: God of mercy, thank you for the cries of the hurting and lost; open our ears to hear them and our hearts to respond in faithfulness to the creation of your realm on earth as it is in heaven. Amen.

Breaking the Silence

Read Acts 18:1–17.

One night the Lord said to Paul in a vision, "Do not be afraid, but speak and do not be silent; for I am with you, and no one will lay a hand on you to harm you, for there are many in this city who are my people." (Acts 18:9–10)

This is a red letter passage. Here are words attributed to Jesus, and they are spoken to Paul in the form of a vision. It's hard to imagine more affirming words from Jesus than this refrain "do not be afraid" or "fear not" spoken by him over 100 times in the scriptures. What is Paul not to fear? Jesus wants Paul to not be afraid so that he can speak openly and preach that Jesus is the Christ.

What if we were unafraid? If Jesus were to come to you tonight in a vision and say these words to you, "Do not be afraid, but speak and do not be silent," what response would rise up in your soul? What would you break the silence about if you were not afraid? Along with fear, shame is often at the root of silence. It takes courage to speak truthfully because often silence covers up difficult issues. We can take comfort in Jesus' promise to Paul, and to us, "for I am with you."

We live in a world where messaging matters. How is your faith community showing up on social media, in the community, and from the pulpit to break the silence about mental illness, for example? Where can your voice be heard on important topics of the day? We speak not simply to hear our own voice, but we speak because it can be a means for salvation. Literally hearing the good news that Jesus, the Liberator, is the Christ is a message of which we need never be ashamed.

Prayer: We praise you and thank you for the assurance that the Spirit of Jesus is with us, granting us courage to break the silence. Amen.

Broken Dreams

Read 2 Corinthians 12:1–10.

But I will go on to visions and revelations of the Lord...he said to me, "My grace is sufficient for you, for power is made perfect in weakness." So, I will boast all the more gladly of my weaknesses, so that the power of Christ may dwell in me. (2 Corinthians 12:1, 9)

For too long the myth of perfection has plagued members of Christian communities, especially ordained ministers. No one is perfect but Christ. Our calling is to follow Christ, not to be confused with being Christ. Here Paul lays it out clearly: God's power is made perfect in weakness. Dreams are broken, visions splinter, and hopes crack. This is what it means to be human, but to be a Christian means that we carry onward, even in our weakness because in that very brokenness—splintering and cracking open—God becomes more visible in the world.

What does it mean that the world can see the power of Christ in our weakness? This notion is contrary to Westernized notions of the competitive marketplace. Often we think that to attract new members, our churches must be as perfect as possible. Yet in this lusting after perfection, something is lost. We risk losing the soul of the church to the marketplace. Christ's grace is sufficient for us. What does that mean for our life together? What does it look like to value grace more than new carpeting in the sanctuary?

Imagine a room filled with the most "imperfect" people in your town, whatever that looks like to you. Now imagine this group coming to your church. If this picture is a stretch for you, why is that so? If not, how did your church become a place that welcomes imperfect people? What would it look like to become a church known for imperfect, weak people filled with the grace and power of Christ?

Prayer: Jesus, teach us to not be ashamed of our weakness and imperfection because it is there in the brokenness that your power is made perfect. Thank you. Amen.

Running Late

Read Luke 1:1–25.

Meanwhile the people were waiting for Zechariah, and wondered at his delay in the sanctuary. When he did come out, he could not speak to them, and they realized that he had seen a vision in the sanctuary. He kept motioning to them and remained unable to speak. (Luke 1:21–22)

The gospel of Luke begins with a vision. The angel Gabriel appears to Zechariah in the temple and says, "do not be afraid" (Luke 1:13). Here the birth of John the Baptist is foretold by Gabriel to his parents Zechariah and Elizabeth. Upon hearing this news, Zechariah remains doubtful, questioning the validity of Gabriel's vision because of the advanced age of him and his wife. He wonders aloud, "How can I be sure of this? I am an old man and my wife is well along in years" (Luke 1:18, NIV).

Outside the sanctuary the people wait. What is keeping Zechariah so long? He is running late, delayed by an encounter with an angel. If the day had gone as he planned, he would have visited the temple, said some prayers, burned some incense, and then gone home. When this ritual is interrupted by an angel appearing before him at the altar, he becomes afraid. He wasn't expecting an encounter with God's messenger in worship.

Imagine that: a vision from God during worship. How many people go to church expecting to see or hear a vision from the Lord? Think about Zechariah the next time you attend worship, and how he was simply going through the motions, thinking about getting home to his wife, when all of the sudden, God's messenger shows up beside the altar. What would you do? Like Zechariah, you may have a difficult time explaining it afterward to your friends. But the proof of it will reveal itself in due time.

Prayer: In our hurried lives as we rush to the next thing, help us to slow down enough to be delayed and surprised by a vision from you. Amen.

Dreaming the Impossible

Read Luke 1:26–38.

"For nothing will be impossible with God." Then Mary said, "Here am I, the servant of the Lord; let it be with me according to your word." (Luke 1:37–38)

Gabriel was a hardworking angel. After his visit to Zechariah, he stopped by Mary's house. His opening line didn't go over well with Mary, as she was troubled with the description of "highly favored." Wasn't that status reserved for kings and priests, for the wealthy and powerful, but not for a poor young woman such as herself? Mary continued to listen to Gabriel, although she remained cautious. Upon hearing that she was to give birth to Jesus, Mary asks a very practical question, "How will this be since I am a virgin?"

Mary knew this was an impossible dream. It could only happen with and from and through God. The angel assures Mary, "for nothing will be impossible with God." From here on out, Mary is on board, trusting that this impossible thing will happen to her because God has chosen her. At the end of this encounter with Gabriel, Mary identifies herself, not in relationship to Joseph her fiancé as she had done in the beginning, but by her relationship to God: She says, "I am the Lord's servant."

Mary is changed completely, not only in her pregnant body, but also in her mind and soul, now fully devoted to the Lord. How often do we encounter dreams for our lives that seem so impossible that we don't even give them a chance to take seed and grow? What if next time we trust that God is present in the impossible and allow ourselves to be transformed?

Prayer: God of small and humble beginnings, open our bodies, minds, and souls to be vessels of your love. Amen.

Visions Stirring Within

Read Luke 1:39–45.

When Elizabeth heard Mary's greeting, the child leaped in her womb. And Elizabeth was filled with the Holy Spirit and exclaimed with a loud cry, "Blessed are you among women, and blessed is the fruit of your womb. (Luke 1:41–42)

The energy in this passage is enough to fuel a revolution. Here we have two women of God, cousins Elizabeth and Mary, both carrying sons that will change the world. Without any verbal disclosure, Elizabeth knows that Mary is pregnant with Jesus. Elizabeth receives this divine revelation because of a vision that originates, not from an angel, but from her own womb. The baby inside Elizabeth's womb "leaps," and her whole body is filled with the Holy Spirit.

Our bodies talk to us every day, letting us know when we are stressed, sick, tired, excited, or afraid. Too often we shut down our body's communication system because we don't want to be bothered by its inconvenient truth or the messages it sends us. Yet listening to our bodies can prevent serious illness and also lead to healing. This story about Elizabeth receiving a vision from her own body reminds us that our physical selves are God's temples too—a place where we can encounter the living God.

Think about your body today. What is your body trying to tell you? Pay attention to how your body feels. Which parts of your body feel energized? Which parts of your body feel drained? Do one thing today that honors your body for the temple of God that it is; it could be something simple like drinking plenty of water, taking a nap or going for a walk. Tell yourself, "I am blessed. I am a child of God."

Prayer: For visions stirring within, Mother God, we give you thanks and pray for healthy bodies to carry your word. Amen.

Visions of Salvation

Read Luke 1:46–56.

And Mary said,
"My soul magnifies the Lord,
  and my spirit rejoices in God my Savior,
for he has looked with favor on the lowliness of his servant.
  Surely, from now on all generations will call me blessed;
for the Mighty One has done great things for me,
  and holy is his name. (Luke 1:46–49)

Mary's song is a powerful testimony to the transformative work of the Holy Spirit. What was once a troubled teen is now a confident mother-to-be. In the presence of her cousin Elizabeth, Mary boldly proclaims the prophecy that will change the world. Her song echoes across the ages, encouraging us with its vision of justice for the poor and radical love for every generation.

Salvation is a rich theological term understood differently throughout the history of the church. Mary teaches us that to be saved is to be seen by God. God looks upon Mary and all of us with favor. Jesus' life, death, and resurrection demonstrate this truth that his mother embodied: God is mindful of us and extends mercy to us. Salvation comes to all who need help. Mary's wisdom transcends our differences and unites us in God's love.

Take a moment to reflect on how you have experienced God's mindfulness and mercy. When have you felt seen by God? What song emerges from your soul in response to God's favor in your life? How can Mary's song be the song of the church today? In what ways can our faith communities be a blessing to the world, sharing God's salvation and mercy, justice and love?

Prayer: God my Savior, thank you for Mary's confidence and courage, wisdom and strength; grant my soul power to sing a song of praise. Amen.

Dreaming with the Saints

Read Ephesians 1:1–19.

I pray that the God of our Lord Jesus Christ, the Father of glory, may give you a spirit of wisdom and revelation as you come to know him, so that, with the eyes of your heart enlightened, you may know what is the hope to which he has called you, what are the riches of his glorious inheritance among the saints, and what is the immeasurable greatness of his power for us who believe, according to the working of his great power. (Ephesians 1:17–19)

"The eyes of your heart" make it possible for every generation to see Christ—to know, hope, and believe in him. We may not see Jesus in the flesh, but we feel his spirit. On this Holy Thursday we join with Christians everywhere by preparing our hearts to see Jesus in his life of service, and in his faithfulness even in death on a cross.

Without a physical encounter with Jesus, not having anointed his feet like Mary Magdalene, or dined with him at the last supper like the disciples, we must depend on our spiritual connection. The saints have shown us the transformative power of a rich spiritual relationship with Jesus, such as the radical faith of slaves in the early nineteenth century, when Jesus helped them escape, making a way to freedom when there was no way. Or the dream that inspired Martin Luther King, Jr. All such dreams are born from God and embodied by women like Sojourner Truth or men like King.

That same spirit of wisdom and revelation in Paul's letter to the Ephesians is available to all of us. As you meditate on Jesus' message to love God and your neighbor as yourself, think about the wisdom of loving and how it is being revealed to you in the passion of Christ.

Prayer: We dream with saints like Martin Luther King, Jr. and Sojourner Truth, whose work and witness brought us closer to heavenly justice; shape our dreams to be full of hope that love wins. Amen.

When Dreams Die

Read Luke 23:44–56.

It was now about the noon, and darkness came over the whole land until three in the afternoon, for the sun stopped shining. And the curtain of the temple was torn in two. Jesus called out with a loud voice, "Father, into your hands I commit my spirit." When he had said this, he breathed his last. (Luke 23:44–46, NIV)

Jesus dreamed: "Blessed are you who are poor, for yours is the kingdom of God. / Blessed are you who are hungry now, for you will be filled. / Blessed are you who weep now, for you will laugh" (Luke 6:20–21). The same Jesus who extended forgiveness instead of vengeance, offered healing instead of judgment, and welcomed all instead of just some to God's banquet table—this same Jesus was arrested, put on trial, and sentenced to death. Did Jesus' blessed dreams die with his body? Did God's dreams for our salvation die on the cross?

How do we reconcile the radical dreams of God alive in Jesus with the rejection and crucifixion of Jesus the Messiah? As people of a crucified God, Christians encounter the brutal realities of the sin that kills God's dream of reconciliation and wholeness. What is the sin that causes such dreams to die? Which sin killed Jesus? Which sin had the power to take Jesus' breath away: injustice. "Darkness" covered the sun, caused by corrupted human hearts focused on destroying God's dream of justice.

God's justice threatens the world's powers and principalities. Jesus is crucified for the poor, the hungry, the sick, the alien, and the outcast. The authorities tried to kill God's dream by killing Jesus. In the shadow of the cross many of the disciples believed that the dream was dead.

We join the women who rest on the Sabbath after preparing the spices and perfumes for his body.

Prayer: God of the darkened sky, when shadows block our view of you and dreams die before our eyes, grant us mercy to watch for glimpses of your returning sun. Amen.

Jesus' Vision Lives On

Read Luke 11:1–13.

He said to them, "When you pray, say:
Father,
hallowed be your name,
your kingdom come." (Luke 11:2, NIV)

Jesus taught many things, but the core of all of his teachings was the vision of God's kingdom come. Jesus' disciples asked him to teach them how to pray; at the heart of the Lord's Prayer is a message about receiving daily bread. Immediately following this passage about prayer, Jesus speaks in parables to convey how generously God gives the Holy Spirit to those who ask.

Today we pause on the day between death and resurrection and we pray for God to give us our daily bread. We ask not only that the physically hungry in our world be fed bread from our abundance, but also that spiritual food be given so that we can forgive those who sin against us and turn away from evil. Without the daily bread of the Holy Spirit, we will not have enough spiritual strength to carry out Jesus' mission of discipleship. Without energy guided by the Holy Spirit to serve, we become lifeless, crucified along with Jesus.

So today we wait with the rest of the world for the proclamation of the good news of God's coming kingdom. We live in the "here and not yet" of God's justice. We stand in the balance of good and evil. We stand at God's door, knocking.

Prayer: Our Father in heaven, hallowed be your name, your kingdom come; give us each day our daily bread; forgive us our sins, for we also forgive everyone who sins against us; and lead us not into temptation. Amen.

Be Thou My Vision

Read Luke 24:1–23.

Moreover, some women of our group astounded us. They were at the tomb early this morning, and when they did not find his body there, they came back and told us that they had indeed seen a vision of angels who said that he was alive. (Luke 24:22–23)

Resurrection begins in the blackness of dark. Night vision is a spiritual power demonstrated throughout the Bible, as reflected in this Lenten devotional referencing many night visions. True to form, we see God's vision of salvation emerging here in early morning, pre-dawn, still dark hours. St. John of the Cross spoke of the dark night of the soul, an experience through the valley of the shadow of death, as the way to spiritual enlightenment. We cannot experience the daylight of Easter without first walking through the dark valley of death.

Yet emerging from the shadows of the cross, and hinted at by the dawning sun, is a renewed vision of glory for God's people. The vision of the Risen Christ greets us this day…hallelujah! As witnessed by the women at the tomb who saw that Jesus' body was not there, and affirmed by the angels who said that he is indeed alive, we are invited to see the vision again as if for the first time.

Today will you raise your spirit with Jesus from the grave, receiving spiritual food from heaven in the form of the Holy Spirit? Will you let your life be resurrected and become a new creation in Christ, receiving the abundance God offers you?

God's dreams and visions live on in each one of us who embraces and follows Jesus Christ, the Resurrected Dreamer. In our dreams and visions, the way forward toward justice, reconciliation, and love becomes known. Will you write down your dreams and visions, make them plain and let them be known so that all may read them?

Prayer: He lives! In God we dream, in Jesus Christ our vision lives, and in the Holy Spirit we breathe; for all this and our journey together, we give thanks. Amen.

NEW *and* FRESH
from CHALICE PRESS

SACRED WOUNDS
A Path to Healing from Spiritual Trauma

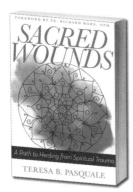

by Teresa B. Pasquale
foreword by Fr. Richard Rohr, OFM

Trauma therapist Teresa B. Pasquale offers healing exercises, true-life examples, and life-giving discussion for anyone suffering from the very real pain of church hurt. Pasquale, a trauma survivor herself, understands the immeasurable value of our wounds once we've acknowledged them and recovered in community. That's why the wounds are *sacred,* and the hope this book offers is a powerful message to anyone suffering from this widespread problem.

Print ISBN 9780827235373

HOLY CURRENCY EXCHANGE

101 Stories, Songs, Actions, and Visions of Missional and Sustainable Ministries

by Eric H. F. Law

Eric Law's foundational *Holy Currencies* (2013) demonstrated a new way ministries can think about the resources needed to do their work in their communities. Law's highly anticipated follow-up book, *Holy Currency Exchange,* shares a variety of tools for thinking differently about how those resources can mobilize ministries into new life, mission, and vitality. Examples include a restaurant ministry, programs for youth, an emergency rent loan fund for people in the neighborhood, worship service in Mexican restaurants, and many more. What could your ministry do?

Print ISBN 9780827215016

chalice press

1-800-366-3383 • www.ChalicePress.com
Ebooks also available

Baptism and Confirmation Resources

Passage into Discipleship

Guide to Baptism

by Christopher W. Wilson

Passage into Discipleship helps older children and youth more faithfully prepare for the act of baptism by teaching what it means to walk a Christian journey. This book incorporates four different learning models that excite young people about becoming followers of Jesus.

Print ISBN 9780827230088

Tour of Life

A Baptism and Confirmation Journey

by Jeff Wright

Tour of Life is an interactive learning experience for youth preparing for baptism or confirmation. It takes youth and their mentors on a journey through the seasons of life, with visits to a hospital nursery, a food ministry, a funeral home, and more to witness God's hand at work in all stages of life. *Tour of Life* draws youth and mentors alike into a deeper faith.

Print ISBN 9780827236615

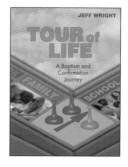

A Travel Guide to Christian Faith

by Dawn Weaks

A Travel Guide to Christian Faith has three components. The *Before You Go* booklet gives first-time seekers an easy-to-understand synopsis of the Christian faith. If they wish to learn more, the *Traveler's Edition* serves as a student workbook, while the *Tour Leader* is used by the instructor.

> "The guide takes travelers from the basic practices of faith, such as how to pray, all the way through baptism, discovering and applying spiritual gifts, and how to create your own 'rule' of spiritual life and holy habits. This set is a must for those churches and church leaders who are serious about helping the barely churched to connect with God, let alone to reaching the growing population of the never-churched." —*Net Results*

Before You Go 9780827217218
Traveler's Edition 9780827217201
Tour Leader 9780827217195

chalice press

1-800-366-3383 • www.ChalicePress.com
Ebooks also available

Books from The Young Clergy Women Project Series

The Young Clergy Women Project (TYCWP) Series features writings from young adult clergy women on topics that give meaning to their lives and ministries. TYCWP includes women from around the world who are committed to serving God and supporting one another. Visit TYCWP online at youngclergywomen.org.

Bless Her Heart
Life as a Young Clergy Woman
by Stacy Smith & Ashley-Anne Masters

Comprising essays from young women clergy, this book is a reflection on the everyday realities of pastoral ministry for the young, female professional.
Print ISBN 9780827202764

Any Day a Beautiful Change
A Story of Faith and Family
by Katherine Willis Pershey

In this collection of personal essays, Katherine Willis Pershey chronicles the story of her life as a young pastor, mother, and wife. *Any Day a Beautiful Change* will strike a chord with anyone who has ever rocked a newborn, loved an alcoholic, prayed for the redemption of a troubled relationship, or groped in the dark for the living God.
Print ISBN 9780827200296
www.katherinewillispershey.com

Making Paper Cranes
Toward an Asian American Feminist Theology
by Mihee Kim-Kort

This theological book engages the social histories, literary texts, and narratives of Asian American women, as well as the theological projects of prominent Asian American feminist theologians.
Print ISBN 9780827223752
www.miheekimkort.com

chalice press

1-800-366-3383 • www.ChalicePress.com
Ebooks also available

COMING HOME

Ministry That Matters with Veterans and Military Families

by Zachary Moon

Coming home from military service is a process of reconnection and reintegration that is best engaged within a compassionate community. Zachary Moon, a commissioned military chaplain, has seen the unique challenges for those adjusting to post-war life. In this book, he prepares congregations to mobilize a receptive and restorative ministry with veterans and their families.

Discussion questions and other resources included will help support small-group dialogue and community building.

Print ISBN 9780827205383

www.ComingHomeChurch.com

ORGANIC STUDENT MINISTRY

Trash the Pre-Packaged Programs and Transform Your Youth Group

by Stephen Ingram

Do you find other youth ministry programs promise you can "plug and play," only to fall short of expectation, forcing you to "adopt and drop"? An organic approach allows each student ministry to exist and live in its best possible way, its natural way! In his book *Organic Student Ministry,* acclaimed youth ministry author Stephen Ingram shows you how to:

- Develop practices instead of just programs

- Minister to students where they are instead of spending your time pleading with them to "get with the program"

- Focus on a way of doing ministry that grows naturally from the distinctively rich and fertile soil of your unique church

Print ISBN 9780827227583   **wwwOrganicStudentMinistry.com**

Help AND HOPE

DISASTER PREPAREDNESS AND RESPONSE TOOLS FOR CONGREGATIONS

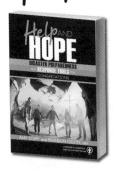

Edited by Amy Gopp and Brandon Gilvin

Joplin. Aurora. New York/New Jersey. Newtown. In times of disaster and tragedy, churches are called to provide sanctuary, hope, and practical aid. Filled with firsthand accounts from disaster-struck communities, *Help and Hope* provides practical instructions for pastors and volunteers who want to prepare now so they are ready when tragedy happens. Designed with utility in mind, *Help and Hope* includes checklists, key websites and contact lists, and space for your own notes. *Help and Hope* prepares you to be shelter from the storm.

Print ISBN 9780827214989

chalice press

1-800-366-3383 • www.ChalicePress.com

Ebooks also available